PRACTICING
GOD'S PRESENCE
24/7

by
Dennis and Dr. Jen Clark

For video demonstrations and further teachings:
www.forgive123.com
www.kingdomlifechurch.us

NOTE: To protect the privacy of individuals in testimonies and true stories, we have given them fictitious names.

www.xulonpress.com

DEDICATION

We dedicate this book to Molly U. Tarr.
Thank you, Molly, for your encouragement, enthusiasm,
suggestions, and support. You have been our dear friend,
intercessor, and sounding board throughout the years.

CONTENTS

"We use our powerful GOD-TOOLS

for...fitting every loose *thought* and *emotion* and *impulse*

into the structure of life shaped by Christ."

2 Corinthians 10:3-6

The Message Bible

PREFACE

Dear reader,

This is a personal letter written to you. I was the first one to embark on this journey with Dennis as my mentor, and it was just the beginning of what has been the most exciting and fulfilling time of my life. I could tell you stories, but I *am* the story!

I am grateful to Dennis for being my husband, my best friend, my pastor, and my mentor. What I learned from him and put into practice in my own life has led to an *Extreme Makeover Jen Edition*. The fruit of this extraordinary transformation has manifested in heart healing, spiritual and physical health, a closer relationship with God, and a newfound purpose in life. I can hardly even remember the pains and fears that were once my constant companions.

My testimony can become your story, too.

What you will learn in the pages of this book were first proven in my own life, but in the past decades these keys have worked for thousands of other people, too. This process works for everyone who wants it. No exception.

This really *works*!

Blessings,
Dr. Jen Clark

I

TOUCHING GOD

The Bliss of Touching God

How long have you been...frustrated...trying to get help...wanting relief from pain...seeking more of God? How is your *hope* level? A little on the low side maybe? Are you weary, longing for the elusive "more", but secretly wondering if this, what you have right now, is all you'll ever have of God-experience? Yet, deep down, in your heart of hearts, a faintly glowing ember–a tiny, fragile spark of hope–still burns.

But, you might say...many have promised so much and delivered so little. You may secretly be tired of church life as you know it. Conferences. Books. Retreats. Yawn! Your problem is that God created you for Himself, for communion with God. And anything short of that leaves you with an emptiness that is never filled.

If what you have tried so far hasn't satisfied, maybe you should try another way!

But discouragement will say, "I already know that. I read the books, took the courses, went to hear anointed preachers."

Wait! What if I told that you are about to learn the secrets of those who discovered the reality of God, the treasures of the Spirit, and...how to make real-life Christianity work? There are hidden truths just waiting to be discovered! Some simple keys that make it all work. Keep reading, because we are about to spill the beans and hand you the keys. All you have to do is be open!

Communion with God is the unspeakably glorious experience for which Christ died—the goal of the Cross.

Christ was crucified and resurrected to open the way for us to *experience* God—His heart, His mind, His will—not just know about Him. When Christ died on the Cross, the veil of the temple was torn from top to bottom, enabling every person on earth to enter God's manifest Presence. This realm of unspeakable love, joy and peace is where we are now invited to live moment by moment, day by day. The

Cross enables us to experience *constant communion* with God and feel the bliss of touching Love Himself.

Does this sound too good to be true? On the contrary: Christ suffered to redeem our lives from darkness and usher us into the glory of His tangible Presence. How dare we settle for anything less?

For centuries, believers from all nations and denominations have sought this magnificent communion with God. Their goal has been simple but radical: the experience of *union*, the sublime joy of uninterrupted relationship, the ever-deepening oneness with the Beloved.

> *The Cross enables us to experience constant communion*
> *and feel the bliss of touching Love Himself.*

We may have read reports of this experience of union with God by saints of old. We may even have heard recent testimonies from pulpits and platforms. But most of us, although we may believe such experiences are true, retreat to our prayer closets and inwardly groan: *How, Lord? When? Where might I find this experience with the Lover of my soul?*

We groan because we know, deep down, that such union is possible, and paid for by the Blood shed at Calvary. We know we were born to experience God. Indeed, the deepest desire of every heart is to experience His Presence—not just occasionally, but moment by moment. Nothing will ever satisfy this deepest need.

We seek His tangible company as one friend cherishes the company of another.

We yearn for His touch as a child longs to be held.

We earnestly desire His embrace even as a bride desires her husband.

Father God desires that His sons and daughters learn how to live like the Biblical patriarch Enoch, who "walked with God." (Genesis 5:24), and like Adam and Eve, who walked with the Lord "in the cool of the day"—but the Cross has afforded us an even *greater* intimacy with God than Enoch, Adam or Eve. The Holy Spirit now resides within us. We can experience oneness with Christ even as Christ experiences oneness with the Father (John 17:11). We can experience abiding in Christ 24/7.

Now is the time for all Christians to learn this most glorious lesson of the overcomer's life: *how to walk in continual communion with God.* We are being called to come into "full stature," to become sons and daughters of God who truly represent Christ to the world.

How does this happen? Through understanding how to touch His Presence, feel His feelings, think His thoughts and do His will—not our own.

We invite you to journey with us into this *experiential union* with Christ. Most Christians believe that this is possible—at least theoretically, doctrinally—but few have actually experienced this intimacy, even momentarily, and even fewer are *practicing God's Presence* all day, every day. But this lesson of communing with Christ is extremely simple to learn; in fact, any child is capable of experiencing this most basic grace of the Christian life. God has already made Himself fully and readily available to the young and the old, the foolish and learned, the broken, the poor, the desperate and the lonely.

> *Communing with Christ is extremely simple to learn.*
> *Any child is capable of experiencing*
> *this most basic grace of the Christian life.*

For many years we have been teaching believers how to abide in Christ and thousands of lives have been transformed. The Lord has healed marriages, physical sicknesses, broken hearts and panic attacks, and has become the ever-present Prince of Peace for many, replacing toxic emotions with Himself.

As we learn to touch God's heart, our emotions will be transformed. And as His divine emotions become ours, the joy of His heart radiating from our lives will draw the lost and broken to the Light of His glory within the children of God. His Presence radiating from within us will bring transformation to nations and revival to the earth.

Communion with Christ is simple and fast, and is summed up in this one word...

Hold on just a minute! Before we tell you what the word is, we must warn you! We are now going to use a word that may *shock* you. It even offends many Christians, as though you are suggesting they have failed to be a model Christian. You may think you know what it means, you may believe you know all there is to know about it. You may even say, "I've already tried that." This is called "being in a box", prejudice, or having a preconceived notion. Set all that aside for a moment.

Picture this. Imagine that you think you have a nice "crystal" paperweight. It is beautiful, but it just sits on your desk unused. What if you suddenly discovered that it was really a flawless diamond. The largest polished diamond in the world is the Golden Jubilee Diamond, 545.6 carats, valued at $4-$12 million dollars. But suppose your diamond is worth billions. That could change everything in your life!

How does communion with Christ happen? *Forgiveness!* Through the most heavenly lifestyle you can imagine—*a lifestyle of forgiveness.* Through learning how to practice forgiveness throughout the day, individuals, families and churches have truly been "born-again again" by experiencing uninterrupted intimacy with God.

Communion with Christ is simple and fast, and is summed up in this one word...*forgiveness.* It could change *everything* in your life! It is not just for salvation, major betrayals and wounds, or for the confessional. It is *the* God tool for maintaining a 24/7 heart connection with Christ.

> *As we learn to experience supernatural forgiveness,*
> *we learn to live in the Presence of God.*

To put it simply: our experience of God's tangible Spirit is blocked or interrupted by our own offenses and sins. To experience Christ without ceasing, we must receive and release forgiveness continually. Most Christians, however, do not know how to forgive. We may *say* we forgive someone who has offended us—but forgiveness is not just saying the right words. We may *pray* fervently with tears—but forgiveness is not just an emotional release. We may even *determine* to forgive by making a quality decision—but forgiveness is not an act of exerting our own will.

Truly, forgiveness is much more than mental assent, feeling sorry, or doing a good deed: it *is a supernatural encounter with Christ the Forgiver.*

This is the secret of communion with God. As we learn to experience supernatural forgiveness—releasing Christ the Forgiver from our innermost being—we learn to live in the Presence of God.

True story*: Kevin, a 26-year-old Iraq war vet, was tormented by flashbacks and recurrent nightmares. While on patrol in Iraq, Kevin's Humvee hit an IED (improvised* *explosive device). The Humvee was blown apart, tearing off Kevin's leg at mid-thigh. His best friend lay dying, his face virtually gone. Debilitating fear and survivor's guilt haunted Kevin from that time on.*

After Kevin returned home to the states, he could hardly keep a job. He was diagnosed with post traumatic stress disorder (PTSD). Irritability, angry rages, nightmares and suicidal thoughts plagued him. His marriage was in shambles. But Kevin learned to yield to Christ the Forgiver and was completely healed and delivered in one prayer session. He had his life back. What had been life-destroying trauma turned to true freedom.

> **Forgiveness is a supernatural encounter with Christ the Forgiver.**

Few of us have experienced the trauma of war, but how often during the day do you feel stressed or offended?

If you're like most people, you probably live with intermittent if not constant anxiety, worry or annoyance. Minor offenses and emotional setbacks—with your spouse, children, co-workers or strangers—are ongoing struggles.

Most of us go to bed with at least a few regrets and wake up with a few worries. We're angered by slow drivers and frustrated in long grocery lines. We feel emotionally spent after long hours at work or months without work. Or we're brokenhearted from a painful marriage or wayward child.

We may have grown slightly weary as we age. We can't stop overeating, overspending, watching TV, surfing the internet, yelling at our spouse or criticizing ourselves. At our most desperate moments, we may even dip into carnality with a few too many beers or a violent movie.

We think we've dealt with our inner demons, wounds and offenses, but continue to feel hurt or frustrated by family, co-workers and friends—and even God.

When we're anxious and stressed, afraid or depressed, it means that *God is not in the equation*. It's not that God isn't present, but that we're not experiencing His tangible Presence because we walk in unforgiveness.

Everyone can learn how to deal with unhealthy emotions and habits and begin to commune with Christ. We don't need willpower, fasting, diets, ministers or even a miracle. We only need to learn this simple way of prayer to *yield to Christ the Forgiver* whenever we feel an offense.

Years ago, Dennis was in our front yard trimming an overgrown bush with manual clippers when a neighbor noticed him struggling. The neighbor took pity and walked over with the right tool—a powerful electric trimmer. "Here, try this instead," he said, laughing. "You've been doing it the hard way!"

The most powerful "God tool" in our spiritual arsenal is the tool of supernatural forgiveness.

The bad news is we have been trying to do Christianity the hard way. The good news is that God has given us efficient, powerful "God tools" for dismantling painful, ungodly emotions and thoughts. Consider this Scripture from 2 Corinthians 10:3-6 in The Message Bible:

"We use our powerful GOD-TOOLS for smashing warped philosophies, tearing down barriers erected against the truth of God, fitting every loose thought and emotion and impulse into the structure of life shaped by Christ..."

The most powerful "God tool" in our spiritual arsenal is the tool of *supernatural forgiveness*. Christ the Forgiver can and will replace every toxic emotion with His peace that transcends understanding. As we learn this simple way of prayer, we begin to learn to abide in Christ.

True story: *Debbie, a 39-year-old divorced woman, lived a life of unimaginable emotional pain because of her past. As a child, she was regularly beaten. As a teen, she was sexually molested. As an adult, she was raped. She'd had three abortions. Finally, she saw her son murdered—and saw the killer walk free.*

Debbie was so traumatized by her history, she had trouble functioning in daily life. But she learned how to present her deepest wounds to Christ the Forgiver and experienced the freedom of forgiveness. In under twenty minutes of prayer Debbie was emotionally healed by the greatest force in the universe. Her sorrow turned to lasting peace. And Debbie excitedly told us that she intended to use what she had learned to help others.

Could Debbie have forgiven her abusers? No, even though she knew it was the right thing to do. Why not? *Only Christ the Forgiver can truly forgive.* Debbie was emotionally healed from her traumatic past because she literally experienced God forgiving her enemies. That's what God does. That's Who God is.

Forgiveness is a supernatural, divine exchange: Christ in exchange for our pain. Debbie learned how to yield to Christ within and let the Forgiver do all the work. Now instead of grief, Debbie yields to God and experiences peace in everyday life by practicing forgiveness.

Few have suffered like Debbie, but we all face pain, fears, and difficulties in life, from the death of loved ones to the daily stress at work, home or school. Our troubles may be relatively minor, but we all encounter stress.

Can this experience of encountering Christ the Forgiver be taught? Absolutely.

For decades, we've helped thousands of average Christians from many denominations and backgrounds learn how to let Christ the Forgiver take their emotional pain and replace it with Himself. We've taught these simple 1-2-3 steps of forgiveness to new believers and seasoned saints; to Protestants and Catholics; Episcopalians and Baptists; charismatics and evangelicals; pastors, priests and nuns; CEOs and PhDs; Goths and millionaires; teens and preschoolers; truck drivers and missionaries.

No pain is too great, no person too damaged or addicted. If you follow these simple steps, you will learn Christ's way of supernatural forgiveness and overcome hurts, fears, lone-liness, anger, guilt, shame and other toxic pathways in your mind and body—quickly and permanently. As we learn to yield to the tangible Presence of Christ the Forgiver, He will displace every painful emotion with His peace.

Communion with God is available to you, no matter what your emotional pain and life traumas have been. This is the unspeakably wonderful promise for which Christ died, the joy that He wants us to know.

> *As we yield to Christ the Forgiver within,*
> *He displaces every painful emotion with peace.*

II

TRUE STORIES

Our own lives have been healed by this same teaching. When Dennis was a new believer, he spent hours simply enjoying the Presence of God in prayer. He longed to bring that same peace with him throughout the day, to experience Christ moment by moment.

God met that desire. More than 30 years ago, the Lord taught Dennis how to *commune with Christ without ceasing* through these simple steps of supernatural forgiveness. Dennis has since lived most of his days in uninterrupted peace. He is able to touch the Presence of God easily, abiding in Christ as he works, drives, eats and rests. And if he ever loses this peace momentarily, he knows how to get it back.

The writings of a 17th century monk, Brother Lawrence, inspired Dennis' spiritual journey. Brother Lawrence provided an example of how to live every moment in unceasing adoration of God. Brother Lawrence called this way of life "the practice of the Presence of God." With every dish Brother Lawrence washed and every floor he scrubbed, he sought to love God and experience His Presence.

Dennis learned, like Brother Lawrence, that prayer was not something that he did, but was Someone with whom he lived in constant contact, no matter the activity.

> *Brother Lawrence lived every moment*
> *in unceasing adoration of God,*
> *the "practice of the Presence of God."*

As Dennis became acclimated to the love nature of God as a young Christian, he began to develop a keen sensitivity to other people. When they were nervous, angry or hurting, he could sense their emotions with his spirit. Despite his growing discernment, however, he still had plenty of hurts, wounds and rejections of his own to battle.

A pivotal moment came the year following his conversion. Dennis had been asked to offer his testimony at a small meeting and was excited about sharing all the Lord had done for him. As soon as he walked on the stage to speak, however, fear and shame so gripped him that he had to leave the platform.

Dennis loved Jesus with all his heart, desired to serve God and had rich experiences in prayer. What was wrong? As Dennis cried out to the Lord in prayer, he saw himself as a young boy with clenched fists, hating himself. It all came rushing back. Dennis had been a bed wetter for many years as a child. He could feel the same shame and hatred toward himself that he had felt as a child decades before. As an adult, Dennis now knew that it was a sin to hate *other* people, but the Lord showed him that it was also wrong for Dennis to hate himself.

Dennis yielded and allowed Christ the Forgiver flow to and through his pain, and Christ replaced Dennis' shame and anger with His supernatural peace. Dennis instantly experienced the Lord touching his heart. The shame lifted and Dennis was flooded with a sense of God's Presence once again.

Dennis learned that *any* toxic emotion *interrupts* practicing the Presence of God, but as soon as he yielded to Christ the Forgiver whenever he encountered an unpleasant situation, a hurtful person or to himself when he needed forgiveness, he returned to communing with God. God *always* showed up to heal him—without fail. Jesus is true to His Word: He *will* deliver us from every one of our pains and sorrows.

> *Any toxic emotion interrupts*
> *practicing the Presence of God.*

The weekend that Dennis and Jennifer met for the first time, before they were married, Jennifer saw Dennis pray with an extremely distraught woman at a Christian conference. The woman, Amanda, had an emotional meltdown and collapsed to the floor weeping. Everyone froze in their tracks. Jennifer was watching, and thought to herself that five or ten years of counseling might help such a broken soul—but this was before she met Dennis and learned these simple steps of forgiveness.

Dennis knelt beside Amanda, who had become hysterical. He began to coach her step by step, walking her through this simple process of supernatural forgiveness. Christ the Forgiver quickly and easily dealt with her emotional pain. In under 10 minutes, Amanda was up on her feet, smiling and calm, testifying that her emotional pain was gone.

Astounded, Jennifer understood that the rapid healing steps she witnessed could bring emotional healing to a world full of hurting people—including the most "mature" Christians still carrying wounds from childhood or battling daily stress at work, in ministry, around the family dinner table or at school. Jennifer realized that whatever Dennis had done was a much faster and more thorough approach than anything she had ever witnessed before.

As a Christian counselor, Jennifer had been very discouraged by the slow progress of her hurting clients. After months, and sometimes years, of prayer and counseling, many sincere Christians continued to suffer from negative emotions. No matter what was tried—classic and innovative therapies, healing and deliverance prayers, Bible instruction—most couldn't experience God's peace and joy consistently and permanently. Some found relief for the short term, but long-term emotional healing was very slow in coming. Even Christians who had been believers for 20 or 30 years continued to suffer from the wounds of the past.

Jennifer's experience was confirmed by many other Christians in the healing professions. A medical doctor who worked with Christians struggling with addictions told her, "I know the Bible says believers are supposed to be new

creations in Christ, but I just see the same old issues."
Experiencing similar failures, another counselor had come
to believe that people had to be fairly well adjusted at salvation or they would be too wounded to ever be "used much"
in Christian ministry.

> *Even the most "mature" Christians*
> *may still carry wounds from childhood*
> *or battle daily stress.*

Jennifer herself was a wounded Christian. Having suffered the death of her first husband from lymphoma, she
struggled to raise her two children on her own, still carrying
emotional wounds from her own childhood and difficult
marriage. Fortunately, God brought Dennis to Jennifer as not
only her new husband, but also as her teacher and mentor in
the ways of supernatural forgiveness.

As soon as they married, Jennifer asked Dennis to teach
her. They began to pray intentional prayers of forgiveness
together regularly, almost daily. Jennifer was not content to
pray through just the major issues in her life, but wanted to
"go for broke". After two months, she found herself marvel-
ously transformed. Jennifer could hardly remember what she

had been like before. Fear was gone. Her emotional pain had been washed away completely. Work was no longer stressful. Life was a delight. Now she knew what the "joy of the Lord" really felt like. Instead of being demanding and controlling, she became emotionally available and trusting. She experienced ongoing peace instead of sorrow and anxiety.

> *Forgiveness has healed and delivered many thousands from emotional traumas, often accompanied by physical healings.*

Jennifer also discovered a deep yearning to teach these secrets of healing and peace to hurting Christians. She had found the "God tool" that not only healed her own hidden fears, anger and shame, but also those of others.

Through forgiveness prayers, Jennifer and Dennis have since seen the Lord heal and deliver many thousands from emotional traumas, mild to severe, often with accompanying physical healings:

- A woman who had been brutally raped answered an altar call for emotional healing and was completely set free from agonizing emotional pain.

- A young man experienced emotional healing and was subsequently healed of color blindness.
- A gifted pianist who was tormented with debilitating panic attacks was instantly healed of fear.
- Another woman experienced an emotional healing which led to a physical healing of a weight problem — and she lost 100 pounds in a short period of time.

Many believers have testified that this simple "God tool" of forgiveness has had profound emotional and physical benefits:

Delivered from chronic shame:

"I carried shame for my entire life. I didn't realize how it colored my world. After learning how to release Christ the Forgiver, I can look people in the eye. I feel freer, cleaner and more whole emotionally than ever before."

Delivered from chronic anger:

"I asked God to root out the cause of my ongoing anger. Immediately, the Holy Spirit showed me scenes of rejection and ridicule by friends and teachers. As each person came to mind, I released Christ the Forgiver to them.

The scenes unfolded in a reverse chronological order, and finally the Holy Spirit led me to the memory of being a bed wetter. My parents made me wear diapers until I was 10 and I endured years of shame and humiliation. I released Christ the Forgiver to myself and my parents. The anger and rejection were replaced with peace—and I'm now filled with incredible joy!"

Delivered from chronic rejection:

"I was completely delivered and healed from a spirit of rejection that plagued me my whole life. Through the lifestyle of forgiveness, I was set free. I now feel *a part* of life and not on the outside looking in. Forgiveness is amazing!"

> **"I have learned to experience continual peace and communion with the Lord."**

Delivered from torment and mere "head knowledge":

"I used to experience much oppression and torment and lived my Christian life in my head. As a result of these simple lessons, I have learned to walk in the Spirit and experience ongoing peace and communion with the Lord. My life has been transformed."

Delivered from deep-rooted bitterness:

"I thought I had totally forgiven everyone in my life but I hadn't. I felt a wall in my gut when certain people came to mind. I had only mentally forgiven them. My emotions were toxic and unchanged. As I learned to yield every pain to Christ within, His peace flowed to my bitterness — and now I live from that peace. This was so liberating that I eagerly do the same with everyone, including myself, whenever anything disrupts my peace."

Delivered from sexual abuse:

"I was severely abused as a child by my father and brother and have struggled for years to forgive, trust and love again. After I released Christ the Forgiver to my abusers, heaven's peace came upon me. The Lord told me to look in Ezekiel 36:26, 'I will give you a new heart and put a new spirit within you.' My new heart feels wonderful!"

Delivered from marital conflicts:

"As newlyweds, we couldn't stop fighting and triggering each others' wounds—but we started to see results the first night we started praying forgiveness prayers. We have grown so much emotionally through this forgiveness lifestyle. With these simple tools, we were not only able to establish a firm foundation for our marriage, but we are also learning to tap into our oneness anointing. Our marriage is truly transformed!"

Indeed, Christ the Forgiver can accomplish a year's worth of therapy in thirty or forty minutes of prayer. The first step to freedom—for ourselves and our loved ones—is in grasping that forgiveness is not a mere doctrine but a Person named Jesus Christ.

III

GOD TOOLS

"We use our powerful GOD-TOOLS for ... fitting every loose thought and emotion and impulse into the structure of life shaped by Christ." (2 Corinthians 10:3-6 MSG)

Forgiveness is a *Person*

Among the last words of Jesus on the Cross are the most powerful words ever uttered: "Father, forgive them." And Father God did just that—forgiving the entire world of every sin ever committed. Jesus died and was risen again to usher in God's unspeakable mercy and forgiveness.

We may believe this Biblical truth in principle, but if we struggle with *any* measure of toxic emotions or stress, from minor worries to deep-seated bitterness, we have not learned how to *forgive others,* nor have we truly learned how to *receive forgiveness* from God for ourselves.

Forgiveness is not just saying the words, "I forgive them, Lord" or "Forgive me, Lord." Mere mental assent is not sufficient. Nor are mere feelings of regret, even accompanied by tears. Heartfelt emotion, however sincere, is not sufficient. Neither is forgiveness a mere decision of our will. We may say, "I choose to forgive them, Lord," but still harbor hurt in our soul

So forgiveness is neither an action of our mind, emotions nor willpower alone, although these faculties are involved. The reality of true forgiveness is this: *forgiveness is a Person.* Forgiveness is an encounter with Someone, a supernatural exchange: Christ Himself for our sin and pain. *We* cannot forgive, as hard as we may try. *Christ* is He who forgives through us. We do not extend forgiveness by ourselves, from ourselves. The apostle Paul writes, "It is no longer I who live" (Galatians 2:20), which suggests that it is also no longer I who loves, nor I who forgives.

> *Forgiveness is a Person,*
> *an encounter with Someone,*
> *a supernatural exchange.*

Christ the Forgiver living inside me does all the work. True forgiveness requires encountering *Christ the Forgiver*, rather than merely knowing and reciting Scriptures or a doctrine of forgiveness.

Consider this Scripture:

*"This is life eternal, that they might **know** thee, the only true God, and Jesus Christ, whom thou hast sent."* (John 17:3 KJV)

The Greek word translated "know" in this Scripture and other Scriptures calling us to "know" God is *ginōskō*. This "knowing" is very different from mere head knowledge or conceptual understanding. This Greek word *ginōskō* means "knowledge grounded in *personal experience.*"

Likewise, the Hebrew word often translated "know" in the Old Testament is *yada'*, as in, *"ye shall know that I am the Lord your God"* (Exodus 16:12 KJV). This Hebrew word also means "to know by experience," personally—also used as a euphemism for marital intimacy.

Knowing Christ, then, must involve personal experience or an encounter, and so it is with knowing Christ as our Forgiver.

> *If you feel **any** unpleasant emotion*
> *when you think of a person, you still need*
> *to experience Christ the Forgiver.*

A husband and wife had a prayer appointment with us a few years ago. When we asked the wife to tell us where she needed to apply forgiveness, she smiled and said, "Oh, I have forgiven everyone in my life!" Her husband looked at her in astonishment and said, "Well, what about your sister and our neighbor? What about forgiving our son for not coming home for Thanksgiving? Or forgiving your mother for always criticizing you and...."

If you feel *any measure* of unpleasant emotion when you think of or visualize *any* person or situation, present or past, then you still need to experience Christ the Forgiver. Ask yourself a few questions:

Do I feel hurt because of what someone did to me in the past?
Do I feel angry about an injustice done to me?
Do I feel intimidated or afraid in certain situations?
Do I put up a "wall" in my gut when you think of certain friends or family members?

If you said yes to any of the above, it doesn't mean that you haven't tried to forgive. It just means that your experience of Christ the Forgiver needs to become personal and experiential. You're not yet emotionally free. It takes complete forgiveness, not partial forgiveness, to deal with these emotions *once and for all*.

Forgiveness is not only required for major emotional traumas and injustices but also for small, everyday irritations and minor offenses we still carry from yesteryear. None of us have resolved every hurt, anger and fear that has happened from childhood through adulthood, but Christ Himself can and will bring to mind old judgments and bitter roots and quickly replace them with His Presence.

> *Forgiveness may begin with a thought, choice or feeling,*
> *but it must end with a God encounter.*

Forgiveness is extremely practical for everyday life. This is what we mean by the *forgiveness lifestyle*.

And it's an extremely easy lifestyle to acquire. Christ the Forgiver is freely available and easily accessible. Forgiveness may *begin* with a thought, choice or feeling, but it must *end* with a *God encounter*. Although we as believers are called upon to forgive, true and complete forgiveness—with lasting results—is divine, not human. It's supernatural, not natural. It's beyond our human ability: it is the grace and desire of Jesus Christ.

Forgiveness is *Required*

Most Christians know that forgiving others is *commanded* by the Word of God, but how many of us harbor small resentments throughout the day? Forgiveness is not optional, even for minor issues. If we do not forgive others, the Bible says, God will not forgive us:

> *"But if ye forgive not men their trespasses, neither will your Father forgive your trespasses."* (Matthew 6:15 KJV)

Only if we forgive others will our Father forgive us (Matthew 6:14). That doesn't mean that we are condemned to hell. It means that we have to live with the torment of our own unforgiveness. Jesus already paid the penalty for our sin of unforgiveness. Forgiveness releases us and others to God so He can work in our lives. In other words, when we allow Christ to forgive through us, we cease to sit in the place of judgment. We release ourselves and others to God, the most just and merciful Judge of the universe.

Only if we forgive others will our Father forgive us.

Failing to Forgive is *Deadly*

The Lord requires that we use this "God tool" of forgiveness, because He also knows the deadly consequences of *when we don't.*

Unforgiveness is like drinking poison to get even with someone else. *Unforgiveness is a trap you make for yourself.*

A recent Gallup poll indicates 80% of workers feel anxious and stressed at work. Approximately 18.1 million adults (13.3% of the adult US population between 18-54 years) suffer from anxiety disorders and panic attacks. And the stress is taking its toll on national health. [1] Studies estimate that 75-90% of all doctor's office visits are from stress-related illnesses and complaints. Stress has become a worldwide plague.

What is at the root of this terrible trend? Unforgiveness. Stress isn't inflicted upon us, but arises when we desire to control circumstances or people, out of fear, guilt, shame, anger or hurts. [2, 3, 4] The root of these toxic emotions is... unforgiveness toward others, ourselves or God. The need to control arises when we doubt God's faithfulness and care, or when we hold unforgiveness toward others or ourselves.

> *Unforgiveness is like drinking poison*
> *to get even with someone else.*

Medical research now affirms that toxic emotions can make us physically sick. In a 2007 *Journal of the American Medical Association (JAMA)* article, researchers from Carnegie Mellon University and the University of British Columbia examined evidence linking the toxic emotion of stress to increased depression, cardiovascular disease and the progression of HIV/AIDS.[5]

Studies link emotional distress to six leading causes of death: heart disease and increased risk for heart attack, cancer, lung ailments, accidents, cirrhosis of the liver and suicide. Research links many health issues with emotions and stress. [6,7,8,9,10] Some conditions associated with or aggravated by stress include:

Back pain	*Headaches*
Chronic fatigue	*High blood pressure and stroke*
Colitis	*Irritable bowel syndrome (IBS)*
Crohn's disease	*Lowered immune system*
Diminished sexual desire	*Peptic ulcers*
Rosacea, eczema, and psoriasis	

Suppressing emotions has negative consequences on health. [11, 12] Research has indicated that chronic anger and hostility may indeed lead to early death. A long-term study showed that people who score in the high range on hostility scales were almost five times more likely to die of heart disease than those scoring lower. Also, they were seven times more likely to die by age 50. [13]

The human body is equipped with a protection system for emergency action in dangerous situations. The body responds by releasing stress hormones for "fight or flight" and an instant burst of strength and endurance. Periodic stress does not harm the body, but ongoing *chronic stress* causes lasting damage.[14, 15, 16] Chronic stress overexposes the body to cortisol and other stress hormones, disrupting the function of the immune system, endocrine system, metabolism, cardiovascular system and nervous system.

True Story: *Shortly after Dennis and Jennifer were married, Jennifer was jerked awake out of a sound sleep by a rapidly racing and pounding heartbeat and a cold sweat. She knew exactly what was happening—paroxysmal atrial tachycardia (PAT). PAT consists of extremely rapid heartbeats that begin and end abruptly. The heart rate suddenly shoots upward to 140 to 220 beats a minute, and feels like it simply won't slow down.*

Jennifer's heart was beating so fast that it felt as if the bed were shaking. This was not a new thing, but a symptom that had tormented her several times a month for the previous 20 years. Dennis woke up and felt the fear flooding the room. He helped Jennifer yield to Christ the Forgiver. Instantly, she felt the fear leave. Her heart immediately stopped palpitating and returned to a gentle, normal rhythm. The atrial tachycardia never recurred.

> **Negative emotions don't die.**
> **We bury them alive!**

The link between stress, anger, fear and disease is not a new discovery—but few experts know how to instantly and permanently heal toxic emotions. If we *don't* deal with stress and toxic emotions in our lives, they lodge in our cellular memory, stored like nuclear waste in a landfill. Suppressed negative emotions *don't go away.* They are just hidden away under the surface of our conscious awareness, like termites secretly eating the structure of a house.

Forgivness is *Proven*

Whereas the terrible consequences of unforgiveness are life-threatening, the tremendous benefits of forgiveness are *life-giving.* Not only does forgiveness free us from being "stuck" in the past, but forgiveness brings profound healing to our heart and great clarity to our mind, to make better decisions based on peace, not anxiety. Forgiveness not only removes barriers that stunt emotional growth, but also spurs intellectual growth: research has proven that stress and anxiety measurably *lower* your IQ!

Forgiveness results in wellness not only of our soul but also of our bodies. Yielding to Christ the Forgiver literally washes the poison of toxic emotions from our cellular memory and allows physical healing to take place. We have witnessed many hundreds of Christians experience physical healings as they forgive others, themselves, and even the Lord Himself.

"If we confess our sins, he is faithful and just to forgive us our sins, and to cleanse us from all unrighteousness." (1 John 1:9)

The Greek word translated "cleanse" here is *katharizō*, which suggests not only moral cleansing but also physical cleansing—the same term used for a leper cleansed of disease.

> *Yielding to Christ the Forgiver*
> *washes the poison of toxic emotions*
> *from our cellular memories.*

Forgiveness may be the best medicine ever discovered by science. Since the 1990's, scientific research in the field of forgiveness has exploded, with many scientific studies affirming its physical and psychological benefits (Lawler, 2003; Lawler, 2005; Worthington, 2001). Studies focus on the emotional, mental and physical benefits of forgiveness as well as the relational and societal implications. Laboratory results document how forgiveness lowers blood pressure, relieves stress, alleviates insomnia, lessens fatigue and leads to better overall health. Many physicians, therapists and researchers—both Christian and secular—are turning to forgiveness for answers.

Forgiveness is the "God tool" that eradicates stress and toxic emotions, heals our bodies and ushers us into "God emotions" that arise through communion with Christ.

Forgiveness is *Simple*

Based on our own observations over the years, it appears that 90-99 percent of Christians do not know how to forgive properly, effectively, and deliberately so that lingering negative emotions are healed permanently. As a result of lingering resentments and fears, we have difficulty experiencing the Presence of God.

Even if some Christians occasionally succeed at forgiving and find emotional freedom, they don't know *what* they did or *how* they did it—and cannot teach forgiveness to others.

Most Christians admit that they take a long time to forgive, and justify the delay by ascribing to the erroneous doctrine that forgiveness is a "process," not instantaneous. Unfortunately, many Bible scholars and preachers have taught that forgiveness often takes a long time. But consider this: was salvation a process or was it instant? As soon as you repented and asked Christ to be your Lord and Savior, He came into your heart. Jesus was immediately faithful to His Word, without delay.

> *We wrongly believe that forgiveness*
> *requires a long process*
> *because we don't know how to forgive.*

When you received forgiveness from Him, did you have to fast and plead? Was it a long process? Not at all! When you were born again, you didn't have to work for forgiveness or beg God for it, you simply received His free gift with childlike faith.

Experiencing forgiveness in our daily lives follows exactly the same course: we call to a *Person* who answers immediately and cleanses us. When you received Christ as your Lord and Savior, you opened your heart to Him and *instantly* experienced salvation, accompanied by peace or joy. And so it is with encountering Christ the Forgiver: He *instantly* replaces pain with His peace—with no "process" required. Consider this Scripture:

> *"As you have therefore received Christ...[so] walk (regulate your lives and conduct yourselves) in union with and conformity to Him."* (Colossians 2:6 AMP)

The word *walk*, translated from the Greek *peripateō*, means the way you live everyday life, how you regulate and conduct yourself and your circumstances. The *way* we received Christ—calling on Him and receiving His response immediately—defines a lifestyle, the *way we walk* moment by moment. We call to Him by faith and He responds!

Could it be that the doctrine that promotes forgiveness as a process originated because we just don't know how to forgive? When we know how to forgive the right way, the process is immediate and permanent, just like our salvation.

Learning how to forgive is vital to every believer, no matter your age, experience or maturity in the Lord. Even as "mature" Christians, most of us still carry wounds and offenses from childhood, family and career disappointments or just daily annoyances, losing God's peace at least occasionally. If we learn to submit every offense to Christ the

Forgiver, we're *guaranteed* to find freedom from emotional pain and learn to abide with the Prince of Peace.

The first step in learning how to encounter the Forgiver is to *locate* our emotions, thoughts, will and heart—so we can then *yield* them to God in exchange for His own.

ENDNOTES

[1] Larzelere, M.M. and Jones, G.N. (2008). "Stress and Health". Primary Care: Clinics in Office Practice. 2008;35(4):839-856.

[2] Worthington, E.L., Jr., Berry, J.W., & Parrott, L. III (2001). "Unforgiveness, forgiveness, religion, and health". In T.G. Plante & A.C. Sherman (Eds.), Faith and health: Psychological perspectives. New York: Guilford Press, 107-138.

[3] Lawler K., Younger J., Piferi R., Billington E, Jobe R, Edmondson K, Jones W.H. (2003). "A change of heart: cardiovascular correlates of forgiveness in response to interpersonal conflict". Journal of Behavioral Medicine, 26, 373-393.

[4] Lawler K., Younger J., Piferi R., Jobe R., Edmondson K., Jones W. (2005). "The unique effects of forgiveness

on health: an exploration of pathways". Journal of Behavioral Medicine, 28, 157-167.

[5] Cohen, S. et al. (2007). "Psychological Stress and Disease". Journal of the American Medical Association (JAMA) 2007; 298(14): 1685-1687.

[6] Jensen, M. (1987). "Psychobiological factors predicting the course of breast cancer". Journal of Personality, 55, 317-342.

[7] Larzelere, M.M. and Jones, G.N. (2008). "Stress and Health". Primary Care: Clinics in Office Practice. 2008;35(4):839-856.

[8] Pennebaker, J. (1992). "Inhibition as the linchpin of health". In H. S. Friedman (Ed.), Hostility, coping, and health. Washington, DC: American Psychological Association. 127-139.

[9] Temoshok, L. (1987). "Personality, coping style, emotion, and cancer: Towards an integrative model". Cancer Surveys, 6, 545-567.

[10] Dennerstein L, Lehert P, Burger H, Dudley E. (1999). "Factors affecting sexual functioning of women in the mid-life years". Climacteric. 1999;2:254–62.

[11] Gross, J., & Levenson, R. (1997). "Hiding feelings: The acute effects of inhibiting positive and negative

emotions". Journal of Abnormal Psychology, 106, 95-103.

[12] Pennebaker, J. (1992). "Inhibition as the linchpin of health". In H. S. Friedman (Ed.), Hostility, coping, and health. Washington, DC: American Psychological Association. 127-139.

[13] Barefoot, J. et al (1984). "Hostility CHD Incidence in Total Mortality - A Twenty-Five Year Follow-Up Study of Twenty Five Physicians". Psychosomatic Medicine, 45: 79-83.

[14] Baum, A. & Polsusnzy, D. (1999). "Health Psychology: Mapping Biobehavioral Contributions to Health and Illness". Annual Review of Psychology, Vol. 50,137-163.

[15] Anderson, N.B. & Anderson, P.E. (2003). *Emotional Longevity: what really determines how long you live*. New York, NY: Viking.

[16] Vgontzas, A.N. et al. (1997). "Chronic insomnia and activity of the stress system: a preliminary study". Journal of Psychosomatic Research, Vol. 45, 21-31.

IV

LOCATION, LOCATION, LOCATION

The number one rule in real estate is *location, location, location*. This same principle applies to spiritual growth. Many Christians struggle with forgiveness and communion with God because we don't understand our spiritual real estate.

Understanding the inner-workings of our *emotions, thoughts, will* and *heart* is the first step in learning to meet Christ the Forgiver.

Locate *Your Emotions and Spiritual Heart*

Most people associate the *chest cavity* with their emotional life and spiritual center or heart, and live out their Christianity from just behind their breast bone. Somehow we have mistaken the Hallmark version of the red Valentine heart for the seat of love, affection and the Spirit of God.

> *Scripture is very clear about our Bible heart.*
> *It's located in our "bowels" or belly area.*

The Bible does not locate our spiritual and emotional centers within our chest but in the *belly* area. This may seem strange—or just a minor detail or mere semantics—but the location of our spiritual and emotional core matters greatly in learning how to use the "God tool" of supernatural forgiveness.

Scripture is very clear about where our emotional center is positioned. The Hebrew term *me`ah* and the Greek *splagchnon,* both translated "bowels," refer not only to the physical digestive organs but also to the location of our emotions, be they feelings of distress, tenderness, mercy or love. This is your Bible heart, the seat of emotion. Consider the use of the term "bowels" in the following Scriptures:

"I am poured out like water, and all my bones are out of joint: my heart is like wax; it is melted in the midst of my **bowels***"* (Psalm 22:14 KJV)

*"Mine eyes do fail with tears, my **bowels** are troubled"* (Lamentations 2:11 KJV)

*"If [there be] therefore any consolation in Christ, if any comfort of love, if any fellowship of the Spirit, if any **bowels** and mercies"* (Philippians 2:1 KJV)

*"Put on therefore, as the elect of God, holy and beloved, **bowels** of mercies, kindness, humbleness of mind, meekness, longsuffering* (Colossians 3:12 KJV)

*"...whoso hath this world's good, and seeth his brother have need, and shutteth up his **bowels** of compassion from him, how dwelleth the love of God in him"* (1 John 3:17 KJV)

Clearly the area of our bowels is the location of compassion, mercy, kindness, humility, meekness, longsuffering — and despair.

Other Hebrew and Greek words referring to our *spiritual heart* are translated *belly*. This belly region comprises the location of God's Spirit within us, from which the Life of God is released:

*"The spirit of man is the lamp of the Lord, searching all the inward parts of the **belly**."* (Proverbs 20:27 KJV)

*"He that believeth on me, as the scripture hath said, out of his **belly** shall flow rivers of living water."* (John 7:38 KJV)

According to the Bible, our spiritual heart or innermost being is not located in our chest, but at our mid-section, within the belly.

"Dropping Down"

Most Christians focus their conscious attention either in their *head* and conduct their relationship with God in their thought life or in their *chest area,* living from their carnal emotions. But if our spirit-heart resides in our belly—not between our ears or within our chest—then we need to *refocus our conscious attention.* We need to shift our focus *away* from our head and chest and *down* to our true spirit-being within our belly. We call this shift of conscious attention *"dropping down."*

By *dropping down,* we pay attention to our belly area—a subtle but ever-so-powerful change of focus. "Dropping

59

down" shifts focus from head to heart. This refocusing of awareness is absolutely vital to our communion with God. Without this shift in attention, we can remain detached from our spirit, living our Christian life through our intellect or emotions alone.

> *"Dropping down" shifts focus*
> *from head to heart.*

Only as we locate our spirit-heart correctly, can we *guard our heart*, as Proverbs 4:23 instructs us, "for out of it flow the issues of life." The Hebrew word *leb* used in this Proverb, translated "heart," occurs almost 600 times in the Old Testament. The term *leb* is very general, referring to many aspects of our being, including our mind, will, understanding, soul, memory, will, passions and the place where we feel courage. The *heart* at our core or mid-section is also where our conscience resides, together with the center of our emotions, moral nature and spiritual life — which, as we have learned in John 7:38, flows out of the belly. Within our heart, we locate the following:

- the seat of grief: John 14:1; Romans 9:2; 2 Corinthians 2:4

- joy: John 16:22; Ephesians 5:19

- the desires: Matthew 5:28; 2 Peter 2:14

- the affections: Luke 24:32; Acts 21:13

- the perceptions: John 12:40; Ephesians 4:18

- the thoughts: Matthew 9:4; Hebrews 4:12

- the understanding: Matthew 13:15; Romans 1:21

- the reasoning powers: Mark 2:6; Luke 24:38

- the imagination: Luke 1:51

- conscience: Acts 2:37; 1 John 3:20

- the intentions: Heb 4:12; 1 Peter 4:1

- purpose: Acts 11:23; 2 Corinthians 9:7

- the will: Romans 6:17; Colossians 3:15

- faith: Mark 11:23; Romans 10:10; Hebrews 3:12

As we can see, the belly is the location of our entire emotional and spiritual heart-life. The wounds of our heart are also located in the area of our gut, not in our chest. Although we may sometimes feel emotional heartache inside our chest cavity, jerk when startled, or get red-faced with embarrassment, the epicenter of the damage is in the belly:

61

"The words of a talebearer are as wounds, and they go down into the innermost parts of the belly." (Proverbs 18:8 KJV)

PRACTICE: *Close your eyes and think of an unpleasant person or situation, current or past. Pay attention to how it feels in your gut. Now, think of a good memory. How does that feel? Can you name the emotion?*

By *dropping down* and refocusing our conscious awareness from our *head and chest* area to our *belly region,* we immediately gain a greater sense not only of our emotions and spirit but also of the Spirit of Christ Himself, Who lives within us.

Locate *Your Will*

Most of us will be surprised to learn that our belly or gut is not only the seat of our spirit and emotions, but also of our *conscience, intention* and *will,* the faculties of choice and decision making. Willpower, self-discipline and self-control are among the most misunderstood and misapplied concepts in the Christian life—leading to a "faith walk" governed by striving, pride and self-effort. Understanding the *location* of our will and how to *yield* our will are two of the most powerful lessons we can ever learn as followers of Christ.

The word *will,* in some translations of the Old Testament, is translated *reins,* or literally our *kidneys.* Our will, that uniquely human faculty of choice and volition, is in our gut—not, as many believe, in our mind, in the brain between our ears.

> **Understanding the location of our will**
> **and how to yield our will**
> **are among the most powerful lessons we can learn.**

Are you unclear about the location of your will? Pay attention the next time a minor inconvenience or offense occurs. You will notice that your gut muscles tighten. You have erected a protective "wall" to guard your heart and exert your own will. If you keep that wall up between you and the person or situation, you will begin to feel stress and anxiety, lose your peace and may notice that the muscular tension increases and spreads—to your back, shoulders, and neck.

This is your willpower at work, trying to control a threatening situation, defend yourself, or keep others at a distance.

> **PRACTICE:** *Try this simple exercise to locate your will. Stand up and allow yourself to fall back a little, but stop yourself. (You may want to try this with your back against a wall.) Where do you feel the stop? You will feel your belly or gut tighten. You stopped yourself as an action of your will. Your volition, or will, is activated in your belly, together with your heart.*
>
> *Now close your eyes and think of an unpleasant person or stressful situation. Pay attention to what you sense in your gut. Notice the increase in tension. Your will actively resists the unpleasant encounter by erecting an invisible "wall" to protect yourself—in your belly.*

Locate *Your Thoughts*

Have you ever heard someone describe a "hunch" or "gut" reaction—or felt a "knowing" in your gut?

We can often find wisdom when we "go with our gut" when making decisions, relying on more than just logic and analysis.

The validity of "gut instincts" is now proven by laboratory research. Scientists and therapists document that our gut, bowels or belly region is the place not only of emotion and will but is also inseparable from cognition or thought. We have *feeling-thoughts*, or "emo-cognitions."

Recent research confirms that we have an emotional "brain" in our gut that is as active and important as the brain between our ears. It is called the "second brain".[1] Experts in neurobiology and psychotherapy have defined a new field of research, *neurogastroenterology* or "enteric neurology".

Although we have a brain between our ears, God has given us a "second brain" with an equally significant function of cognition, or *knowing*, in our gut. Have you ever heard anyone use the expression "I *know* that I know"? There are two places of knowing. This second brain is called the "enteric nervous system."

There are as many neurons in the enteric nervous system as there are in the brain and central nervous system. Millions of neurons line the walls of our esophagus, intestines, stomach and colon. Our two brains interact by way of the "left vagus nerve" connecting the emotional center in the brain, the limbic system, directly to the intestines. Neuropeptides are released throughout the body and brain, transmitting emotional information to every cell, organ, and system of the entire body.

> *"I know that I know"*
> *There are two places of knowing!*

We can witness the validity of "gut responses" in a new type of polygraph test. The traditional polygraph assessment collects physiological data from at least three systems in the human body including respiratory activity, sweat gland activity, and cardiovascular activity. Unfortunately, it is possible to beat a polygraph. There is plenty of information out there teaching people how to do just that. Dr. Pankaj Pasricha and his team at the University of Texas recently measured nerve activity in the stomachs of volunteers, asking some individuals to lie and others to tell the truth.[2] The "liars" were discovered by measuring reactions in the gut. Dr. Pasricha observed, "The gut has a mind of its own. Its nervous system acts independently." In other words, this is a polygraph system that is completely reliable. In 2008, Dr. Pasricha applied for a patent for a new type of lie detector based on his research.[3]

Now we can understand why we will immediately *feel* an emotion, often in our belly area, when we *think* about a painful experience or *imagine* a hurtful person. Our two "brains" are experiencing the memory at the exact same time. It is *as* important to attend to the thoughts or images in our head *as it is to feel the emotions in our "bowels."* Suppressing negative emotions associated with thoughts only buries them deep in our unconscious, making communion with Christ more and more difficult. Christ the Forgiver wants to cleanse toxic emotions from every cell and every neural pathway.

> **It is as important to attend to the thoughts or images in our head as it is to feel the emotions in our "bowels."**

Locate *What or Who is "Ruling"*

If our own soul rules, we will think our own thoughts, feel our own feelings and choose to do our own will. If we yield to Christ within, His thoughts will become our thoughts. His feelings will be our feelings His will becomes our will. In other words, God's *revelations* will rule over our mind. The *conviction and direction* of the Holy Spirit will guide our will. And *Christ's heart* will transform our emotions to be His own.

"...let the peace of God rule in your hearts..." (Colossians 3:15)

Christ desires to rule over every part of our being so we can be "set apart" for the Lord. This is the process of *sanctification.*

Many Christians attempt intentional sanctification in the wrong manner. In an effort to renew our minds and calm our troubled emotions, we try to push or force-feed the Bible from our head to our heart, and often call this process "meditating on the Word." Most believers will admit that this process is ineffective, despite good intentions. We may know the Bible "by heart" and earnestly quote Scriptures about peace and joy to renew our mind, yet we may still battle stress, anxiety and fear, harboring resentment and tossing at night.

> *Sanctification is the process of*
> *Christ ruling over every part of our being—*
> *through our yielding to Him.*

Anti-depressants and cognitive or behavioral therapies are popular secular alternatives for emotional healing, and may indeed be somewhat effective for a season, but the root issues of the spiritual being will remain unchanged.

Willfully changing our minds or habits through talk therapy or self-discipline, or altering brain chemistry through drugs may alleviate or lessen our symptoms and offer much needed relief—if not life-saving intervention—but ultimately only Christ the Forgiver will bring permanent freedom, peace and joy. Only *Christ Himself* can bring new life to a broken soul, and the Life of Christ *flows out* from our belly, our innermost being—not our minds, nor our willpower.

Consider this well known Scripture:

"Do not be conformed to this world, but be transformed by the renewing of your mind that you may prove what is that good and acceptable and perfect will of God." (Romans 12:2)

The Greek term *nous*, translated "mind" is more accurately rendered "mindset," which includes the entire soul, the thoughts, will and emotions—or our ability to think, choose, and feel. In other words, our entire *soul* needs to be transformed, not just our cognitive processes or thoughts.

In order to be transformed in the Biblical sense, we need to have a renewed soul. We must face and feel *every* emotion that arises, without denial or avoidance, to give the Lord the opportunity to bless that emotion as honoring Him, or cleanse that emotion as a wound in our soul. The Holy Spirit will transform our soul—our thoughts, will and emotions— as we *yield to* Christ the Forgiver within.

> **The Holy Spirit will transform our soul—our thoughts, will and emotions—as we yield to Christ the Forgiver within.**

Some Christian teachings wrongly encourage us to disregard or subdue our emotions by sheer willpower or by "applying the Word" to our situation. On the contrary, *paying keen attention to negative emotions,* as painful as they are, is an essential part of abiding in Christ and practicing the Presence of God. Once we learn the secret of releasing forgiveness, we'll see negative emotions as marvelous opportunities to experience Christ the Forgiver all over again. Allow your emotions to become your friends! Your emotions tell you whether or not Christ is ruling at any given moment. When He rules our lives, we feel peace.

We make forgiveness difficult when *we* try to do what *only God* can do. *Let the One who forgives sins take control.* You somehow managed to cooperate when you were born again. Was that hard? No: you simply *yielded* your heart and received forgiveness from Christ the Forgiver. Christ is the Forgiver so forgiveness works every time, without fail.

$$\left\{ \quad \textbf{\textit{Allow your emotions to become your friends!}} \quad \right\}$$

It's important to remember that there are no "big or little" offenses to forgive. No matter the severity or history of the issue, every wound is easy for Jesus to heal! Some believers feel that sanctification — our soul being set apart for Christ — is not necessary. Or, if it is, that it is a "sovereign" work of God that has nothing to do with us. On the contrary, sanctification must be intentional. The Bible exhorts us to "be ye transformed by the renewing" of our soul (Romans 12:2), which suggests that it is our responsibility as Christians to participate. How do we collaborate with God in intentional sanctification without exerting our willpower, striving or trying to be holy?

71

The next important step to learn is the easiest "how to" of all: we must learn how to *yield,* to let go, and welcome Christ the Forgiver to do His sanctifying work in our souls.

ENDNOTES

[1] Gershon, M. (2003). *The Second Brain.* New York, NY; HarperCollins. (Original work published 1999).

[2] Parischa, P. (2005). "The stomach cannot lie". New Scientist. Magazine, issue 2524, 05.

[3] Parischa, P. (2008). "Lie detection via electrogastrography". US2008/0177157 A1. Houston, TX.

V

THE GRACE OF YIELDING

As explained, understanding the *location* of our will and how to *yield* our will are two of the most powerful lessons we can ever learn as followers of Christ. Now that we understand the location of the will in our gut, we can learn to yield and allow Christ the Forgiver to flow like a river from our innermost being.

> *Yielding our will*
> *activates Christ's Presence within us.*

As we "drop down" and refocus our conscious attention to our belly region, we will begin to discern our emotional state and the condition of our will. We may feel a negative emotion when recalling a painful situation. Or we may feel tension in our gut when our will is defending us against a threatening situation or person.

Yielding our will activates Christ's Presence within us. We yield, He works. His Spirit indwells every believer and, as we read in Philippians 2:13:

*"... it is God who is **at work in you**, both **to will** and **to work** for His good pleasure."* (Philippians 2:13 NASB)

Christ is near, in your heart! Distance is a deception. God is in heaven, of course, but He is also with you. It is one of the spiritual mysteries. The Bible says that we can know God as our *Immanuel*, or "God with us" (Matthew 1:23):

*"**Christ in you,** the hope of glory"* (Colossians 1:27)

*"The kingdom of God is **within you**"* (Luke 17:21)

How exactly do we yield our will and let Christ within... *flow out?*

"He that believeth on me, as the scripture hath said, out of his belly shall flow rivers of living water." (John 7:38 KJV)

The "Door" of Our Will

We "open the door" to welcome Christ when we are born again, but we must also learn to *yield* to Christ and allow His Spirit to have dominion in our soul on a daily basis. Consider this Scripture:

"Behold, I stand at the door and knock. If anyone hears My voice and opens the door, I will come in to him and dine with him, and he with Me." (Revelation 3:20)

Imagine hearing a car pull up at your house and seeing your least favorite person walking to your front door. You put up an *inner wall* in your gut with your will, closing the door of your spiritual heart—also located in the belly, as we have learned—and protecting yourself.

Your willpower has taken over to control an unpleasant circumstance. You close the door to protect your emotions.

> *We can choose whether or not*
> *to open the door of our will*
> *and let Love enter—and then flow out.*

The heart in your belly has a *door* that gives God and other people access—or not. That door to our heart is our *will*. When you are suspicious about someone's motives, you close your heart to them and stop being vulnerable: your *will* shuts the door of your heart. When you feel tension in your gut, you know that your willpower has been engaged. You're willfully closing the door.

Now, it is important to remember that you open to Christ within. You don't open to other people. That way you are still *open*, but the peace of God is armor: peace protects, or guards, your heart and your mind. In Ephesians 6:15, we are instructed to put on armor, to wear *shoes of peace*. When peace is guarding us, it is like having a super strong screen door. The fresh air can circulate, you can feel the breeze, but mosquitoes can't come in.

"...the peace of God, which surpasses all understanding, will guard your hearts and minds through Christ Jesus." (Philippians 4:7)

As we read in Revelation 3:20, Jesus says that He stands at the door of the heart and knocks, waiting for us to open to Him. We can *choose* whether or not to open the door of our will and connect with Love inside — and allow Love Himself to flow out. It's a matter of yielding our will and letting the door swing open. That door is what opens for Jesus when we are saved. That door of our will in our belly is also the "valve" that can open or shut off the connection with God in the daily life of a believer.

Our relationship with God is not a matter of thinking about the Lord, analyzing Scriptures or saying mental prayers — but an act of our will to *open the door* of our heart! Consider what Jesus said about mere "head knowledge" of Him:

"You have your heads in your Bibles constantly because you think you'll find eternal life there. But you miss the forest for the trees. These Scriptures are all about me! And here I am, standing right before you, and you aren't willing to receive from me the life you say you want."
(John 5:39-40 MSG)

The Bible, however, says that God is a *spiritual* being and those who worship Him must approach Him in *spirit* and truth (John 4:24 AMP). The connection with God must be made by our spirit, not our intellect. Heart not head! Thinking about God is *not* the same thing as having an experiential encounter with Him:

> *"Your worship must engage your spirit in the pursuit of truth. That's the kind of people the Father is out looking for: those who are simply and honestly themselves before him in their worship. God is sheer being itself—Spirit. Those who worship him must do it out of their very being, their spirits, their true selves, in adoration."* (John 4:23-24 MSG)

> **The connection with God must be made by our spirit, not our intellect. Heart not head!**

Our will is the valve, or door, into the spirit. As we yield our will to God we open a spiritual connection to the Presence of God. He lives in our spirit-man, in our innermost being, not in our head or carnal emotions.

Drop Down and *Yield*

We now understand that it's vital to open the door of our heart, located in our belly, by yielding our will. A yielded will opens the heart to Christ.

Remember the earlier exercise of standing up and letting yourself fall back slightly? When you stopped yourself from falling, you exercised the faculty of your will (in your gut) to control yourself. That same will is what you need to *release or relax* in order to contact your spirit.

"Dropping down" to Christ in your heart means refocusing your conscious attention away from your head, down to your belly region, to make a spirit connection to *Christ within*.

Again, *Christ within* is not in our chest cavity, but in our innermost being down in the belly area.

We simply open the door of our heart (located in our belly) by *relaxing our will*. This relaxation feels a bit like relaxing your abdominal muscles. When we relax our will, the door of our heart opens, and living water from Christ within flows out from our spirit.

Does this sound too *mechanical* to be God?

Does God really inhabit a certain place in our body?

In fact, the Lord is King over all of us, body, soul and spirit—but some parts of our being are not yet set apart for His use. Meaning, they're still wounded and confused, and filter our experience of God. When we "drop down" and connect with God in our spirit, focusing on our belly, we are no longer relying on our mind or emotions to communicate with Christ within or experience His Presence.

> *When we "drop down" and relax our will,*
> *the door of our heart opens and living water*

The mechanics of "dropping down" to focus on our spirit in our belly is a method for helping believers identify the spirit-faculty given to us by God, through which we worship Him and abide in Christ.

Connect with *Christ Within*

As soon as you "drop down," yield your will and open the door of your heart. You will instantly make a connection to God in your spirit and feel His peace. When we open the door of our heart, Christ promises to have fellowship with us, no matter what. He always arrives.

If you then start thinking about your "To Do" list, all the worries and responsibilities of your day, you will feel a mild anxiety. But as soon as you "drop down" again and connect with God spirit-to-Spirit in your belly, the anxiety will leave and peace will return. Your worries will fade.

PRACTICE: *Place your hand on your belly. Drop down and focus on Christ within. Relax your will by leaning back a bit, rocking back on your heels. Or, you may want to lean back slightly against a wall. Don't think or try to feel anything. Just be aware of Christ within you.*

Relax your will, almost like a "cuckoo clock" door opening in your belly. You will immediately notice His Presence, and His peace, coming from deep within you. Bask in His love.

"Dropping down" and yielding your will are skills that can be learned and developed with practice. Once we learn to open to Christ within, the next step is learning how to abide with His peace, His *shalom,* without interruption.

The *Shalom* of God

What is *peace,* the English translation of the Hebrew word *shalom?* God's *shalom* is the absence of conflict, a deep, inner tranquility. It is defined by completeness, safety, health, prosperity, quiet, contentment and welfare. *Shalom* is the absence of stress, anxiety, fear, resentment or worry. The Bible clearly states that we are not to fear, to cast all of our cares on Him, and not to worry about *anything*:

"Don't worry about anything; instead, pray... Then you will experience God's peace, which exceeds anything we can understand. His peace will guard your hearts and minds as you live in Christ Jesus." (Philippians 4:6-8 NLT)

As soon as you connect to Christ within, internal conflict will dissipate and you will feel peace—sometime gentle, at other times profound.

> **Shalom** *is the absence of internal conflict—*
> *the deep inner tranquility of Christ Himself.*

God's extraordinary peace and the joy that follows are the manifestations of the love of God described as "the fruit of the Spirit."

"The fruit of the Spirit is love, joy, peace, longsuffering, kindness, goodness, faithfulness, gentleness, self-control [temperance]." (Galatians 5:22-23)

The *God Emotions!* We experience God Emotions flowing through *our* emotions as the fruit of the spirit! God is an *emotional God*. He doesn't just *have* love, He *is* Love. He doesn't *have* peace, He Himself *is* peace. He *is* joy.

> *We experience God Emotions flowing through our emotions as the fruit of the spirit!*

God's peace is "the peace that surpasses all understanding" (Philippians 4:7). This word *understanding* comes from the Greek word *nous*, which includes *thoughts, choices,* and *emotions*. God's supernatural peace is supremely better, higher, and more excellent than anything that comes from our human thinking, choosing, or feeling.

"Peace I leave with you; my peace I give you. I do not give to you as the world gives. Do not let your hearts be troubled and do not be afraid." (John 14:27 NIV)

To "yield" to Christ means that you open your heart, yield your will and surrender yourself into His arms of love, trusting that God is faithful to care for you, no matter what.

Babies yield themselves when they fall asleep in their mother's arms.

Lovers yield to each other's arms.

It's a place of ultimate, total trust, rest and loving assurance.

When you relax your will and yield to Christ moment by moment, you let go of the need to control people or situations through your intellect or will.

It's a lifestyle of radical trust.

Yielding feels a little bit like being so relaxed you could fall backwards into someone's arms if you allowed yourself to do so. With practice, you can gradually become a wholly yielded vessel, letting go of willpower, agendas and self-assertion, open to the love and peace of God flowing in and through your spirit. This is what it means to practice the Presence of God. With practice, your perception of slight changes in the spiritual atmosphere can become finely tuned. You will begin to distinguish subtle movements of the Holy Spirit. You'll notice that the Presence of God feels stronger at certain times than others. When you read the Bible, you may notice an increase in God's Presence in your belly as you linger over certain verses. That means the Lord wants to speak to you through that particular word.

The key is maintaining an *awareness* and *yieldedness* to God's Spirit within, then yielding *more and more*. There is no end to the depths of just how surrendered we can be to the marvelous love of Christ within!

The next step is to learn to yield, to maintain communion with God by yielding to Christ the Forgiver in prayer, in everyday activities, and *whenever* any negative feeling or thought arises. That takes commitment and practice. Practice makes...permanent!

"... solid food is for the mature, who because of practice have their senses trained to discern good and evil." (Hebrews 5:14 NASB)

> *Practice makes...permanent!*

Communion *without Ceasing*

If your thoughts turn to worries and fears, your attention and affections drift away from Christ and you are no longer focused on the spirit. You will no longer feel the peace of God. As soon as you notice you are not feeling peace, "drop down" and return to Christ within.

PRACTICE: *Place your hand on your belly to help you focus. Sit down, close your eyes and imagine that "door" opening in your belly as you relax your will. Inside, you should feel "open." This is what it feels like to yield your heart to the Lord. His Presence, and His peace, will flood your heart.*

Now think of a concern, offense or worry, or picture someone who hurt you. Notice that you feel God's peace diminish and stress return. "Drop down" again and yield your will. Release any troubling concern into the hands of God. His Presence and His peace, will return without fail.

It's a simple formula: if you "drop down" and yield to Christ, you will experience the peace of God. If you're living in your head or through your emotions, you will live in an undercurrent of mild to strong anxiety when negative thoughts or emotions arise. Notice the difference between yielding or opening your heart to Christ and not yielding.

> *It's simple: if you "drop down" and yield to Christ, you will experience the peace of God.*

This may be wonderful in theory, you may say, *"But emotional pain and negative thoughts bombard me throughout the day! How can I abide in Christ when I can barely function?"*

This is the marvelous secret *of supernatural forgiveness,* an easy 1-2-3 process to releasing Christ the Forgiver, explained in the next section. It is not a *method* any more than the "Romans Road to salvation" is a method. It is an *explanation of a spiritual process* that "demystifies" a walk in the Spirit.

VI

FORGIVE 1-2-3

O ne definition of prayer is *spiritual communion.*
Another way to think of communion is *heart connection.* When you are really involved with another person
relationally, you genuinely care for them.

Hearts become *knit* together.

Mothers *bond* with babies.

Lovers *bond* in marriage.

God wants to *bond* with us, spirit-to-Spirit, heart-to-Heart.

But there are roadblocks along the way on our part. The
Bible says that we have the ability to open and shut the door
to our hearts.

"...whoever has this world's goods, and sees his brother in need, and shuts up his heart from him, how does the love of God abide in him?" (1 John 3:17)

As long as the door of your heart is *open* to God, you can experience His Presence. If you are worried, stressed, angry, or preoccupied with the cares of life, however, you have *closed* the door of your heart with your will and will no longer experience His Presence. He hasn't moved away, you have!

In both the Old and New Testaments, the Lord promises that "He will never leave you and never forsake you," but you can lose your Christ-awareness temporarily. If you move away from your spirit and focus on fears and worries, you will no longer experience His Presence, although He is still near. You are simply choosing, by your will, to rely on your own strength and go it alone. The alternative to relying on ourselves is to *yield our will*, open the door of our heart and choose to abide in Christ within.

> *If we're stressed,*
> *we've closed our heart with our will*
> *and no longer experience the Presence of God.*

First, Feel, Forgive

First, feel, forgive.
First, feel, forgive.
First, feel, forgive.

These are the three simple steps to abiding in Christ without ceasing: FIRST, FEEL, FORGIVE. If you follow this 1-2-3 process, you will be healed and made emotionally whole in a very short time—and remain healed. You'll carry the peace, love and joy of the Lord wherever you go, sharing God's manifest Presence with the hurting and lost—rather than just trying to keep your own head above water and out of stress, worry and despair.

Are you ready to be free?

> **All we have to do is present the pain to Him,**
> **yield—then allow Christ the Forgiver**
> **to wash away our toxic emotions.**

We promise that this process will work for you, no matter how deep and longstanding your emotional pain. These three easy steps have been developed over decades of ministry. We have never been disappointed: the Lord Himself has shown us that He *never* refuses to cleanse a heart that is filled with pain.

All we have to do is *present the pain to Him*, yield and allow His forgiveness to wash away any toxic emotions. Freedom is that easy.

First, get comfortable. Find a quiet place to sit alone with God, without the distractions of cellphones, e-mails, friends or family. This is *your time* to meet with the Lord. He longs to meet with you—and is already closer than your breath.

It helps to close your eyes and put your hand on your belly, the location of your heart.

Now, "drop down," as you have learned in the previous pages, and focus on Christ within. Open the door of your will and yield to God. By "dropping down" and opening to Christ, you are inviting Him to work in you.

You're ready to begin Forgive 1-2-3.

FORGIVE 1-2-3
1. "FIRST"

Invite the Lord to bring to mind some circumstance or relationship where there is a need for healing. Focus on the *first* person or situation that comes to mind. You may see a picture in your mind's eye or a short "movie clip" of a moment in the present or past.

> **Trust your loving Healer to bring to mind whatever He feels is most important.**

Don't dismiss or overlook *any* picture or memory that seems insignificant or random. God knows what is important—and also knows the best order in which to proceed. Most often, the issues that *seem* small to us have tremendous significance in our lives. *God knows best.* Trust Him to bring to mind whatever He feels is most important.

It may help to think of yourself as a child who needs help. Go to your heavenly Father with childlike faith, simply trusting that the "first" person or situation that comes to mind is truly from an all-knowing, all-loving God who is powerful enough to communicate with you clearly and directly.

2. "FEEL"

Next, get in touch with the feelings in your gut. "What do I *feel* when I think of or imagine this person or situation that just came to mind?" Every thought has a corresponding emotion. *All* thoughts are *feeling-thoughts*, or *emo-cognitions*.

Pay attention to the negative *emotion* you feel in your belly area. Don't think, but *feel*. Pay close attention to your gut. When you think of that person or situation that God brings to mind, what is going on inside your belly?

$$\left\{ \quad \textbf{\textit{Every thought has a corresponding emotion.}} \quad \right\}$$

You don't even have to "name" the emotion. It may be very subtle or extremely strong, from a vague, nameless discomfort to more obvious rage or sorrow.

You only have to feel the negative emotion *momentarily*. God does not require you to feel the full extent of your emotions in order to receive healing. There is no reason for you to dwell on the feeling or plumb its depths. Just experiencing "the tip of the iceberg" of an enormous feeling is sufficient — no more.

What if feeling a particularly painful emotion seems more than you can handle? Remind yourself that feeling *a moment of discomfort* is a small price for a lifetime of peace and freedom in that area. Let the feelings arise as much as possible. Christ can work with *whatever* area of brokenness you offer Him, no matter how small, confused, painful or undefined. All you need, remember, is a *mustard seed* of faith.

> *A moment of discomfort is a small price*
> *for a lifetime of peace and freedom.*

As you think of or imagine the person or situation God brings to mind, what does it feel like *inside you?* That emotion has been in you all along, even if the emotion was hidden. It has been lurking beneath your conscious awareness. Unresolved emotions are stored in the brain's long-term memory and in the cellular memory of the body, but God will bring to the surface what He wants to heal, in the best order.

3. "FORGIVE"

Always start with the emotion. While you *continue to feel the feeling,* "drop down" to focus on your spirit and yield your will, opening the door of your heart. Yield to Christ within, and allow a river of forgiveness to flow toward the person who provoked the negative emotions, or receive forgiveness for yourself.

Forgiveness is complete when the *negative emotion changes to peace*. Christ Himself will bring healing to that wound in your heart—and to your cellular memories and neural pathways—with His very Presence, and give you peace.

Forgiveness flowing out from your innermost being actually feels like *a gentle river of love* rushing out from inside your belly toward that person or situation the Lord wants you to forgive. Let His river flow *until the pain, or fear, or anger changes to peace*.

Then and *only then* has that unforgiveness been cleansed by Christ Himself.

That's your sign of forgiveness: *your pain has changed to His peace*.

The most important question is whether or not you feel peace inside when you think of the person or situation again. You never have to guess if you did it right. Close your eyes, drop down, picture the exact same situation or person again, and you should feel peace, permanent peace. If you can see that person who offended you or return to the memory and feel peace instead of pain or bitterness, then forgiveness is complete.

> *The sign of forgiveness:*
> *your pain changes to peace.*

If, on the other hand, you picture the person or situation and feel *even a twinge of negative emotion,* then return to the process of dropping down, yielding your will and releasing Christ the Forgiver. Keep releasing love until the emotion turns to peace.

Remember, Christ the Forgiver is the One who does the forgiving. There is *nothing for you to do but yield* and let His river of love flow through you.

It is extremely important that you pray through *only one* memory or vision at a time, and pray through each emotion, releasing Christ the Forgiver *until you feel peace.*

Be patient with whatever God presents to you, in whatever order, no matter how "random" it seems. *Sequence is important,* so always go in God's order, according to His leading. He is aware of the larger structures of your soul and understands how to dismantle strongholds wound by wound, in the most effective sequence.

> *There is nothing for you to do but yield*
> *and let His river of love flow through you.*

Forgive in Three Directions

Often you have to forgive in more than one "direction." Forgiveness may be directed toward another *person* or *situation,* but it can also be directed toward *God* and *yourself.* Why? Perhaps you've held on to regrets from the past or held judgments against others. You need to let Christ the Forgiver cleanse *you* of those regrets and accusations. When we hold unforgiveness, it's a sin.

Maybe you feel guilt and shame about things you've done *or* haven't done, sins of omission or commission. Simply open your heart, yield your will and let Christ the Forgiver flow *toward yourself,* cleansing you of sin.

> *Forgiveness may be directed*
> *toward another person,*
> *God or yourself.*

Maybe you've accused God of withholding blessings from you. You've grown bitter and disappointed by hopes that were deferred. Once again, open your heart, yield your will to *Christ the Forgiver. Allow forgiveness to flow out, toward God Himself.* Also receive forgiveness *toward yourself* for holding a grudge against the Lord.

A person who was abused, for example, might be angry at the perpetrator, blame themselves for not stopping it somehow and feel hurt by God because it was allowed to happen. That person can open their heart, yield their will and let Christ the Forgiver flow in three directions—first to the perpetrator, then to themselves and then to God.

If in doubt, forgive in all three directions—toward others, yourself and God—because you can't forgive too much.

"FACT"

THIS IS VERY IMPORTANT: Most of the time *there is no lie*, or stronghold, that needs to come down! Lies come in at the time of emotional wounding, but the vast majority of emotional wounds do NOT have a lie attached. In our experience, only about one out of every 20 or 30 emotional healings has a lie attached. Therefore, we *always* start with the emotion. When you deal with a negative emotion through forgiveness and have peace, you have the spiritual authority to deal with a lie! Peace is the place of power!

{ ***When you have PEACE***
you are in the place of POWER! }

After you forgive, if there is a lie, it will immediately come to mind. You don't have to guess, search for it, or analyze. You will know.

Now that you are experiencing God's *shalom* and receiving His revealed truth, you are in an the place of spiritual power, or authority, to *pull down strongholds* in the name of the God of Peace. Why? Because "the God of Peace shall bruise Satan under your feet" (Romans 16:20). Spiritual warfare and intercession done from the *position of peace* through the Prince of Peace are infinitely more powerful and effective than contending and striving in prayer with an anxious, troubled spirit.

Renounce any lie that contradicts God's Word or His loving Nature, yield once more and let Christ the Forgiver flow into your innermost being. Now, wait, allow the Lord to show you the truth. *"What do You say, Lord?"*

God's truth is scriptural FACT! A scripture or scriptural phrase will come to mind immediately. Receive God's truth and then say the truth out loud. Factual truth will replace the lie. Write it in your journal! Use the *facts* spoken to your heart by the Lord to declare God's truth about yourself, your situation or another person.

> **God will not contradict His Word or His Nature.**
> **"What do You say, Lord?"**

Receive God's truth with gratitude and cherish His Word in your heart and soul. Allow Him to write it on the tablet of your heart. Then *decree* the will of the Lord from the place of peace, casting down strongholds "and every high thing that exalts itself against the knowledge of God" (2 Corinthians 10:5).

"FILL"

If a lie came to mind, deal with that. Once you have received a revelation of God's *facts* regarding your situation and cast down the strongholds and lies you held dear, allow Him to *fill* you with His Holy Spirit.

> **What is the goal of all forgiveness?**
> **To be filled with Christ Himself.**

Simply drop down, yield your will and open your heart to receive more of Him! He longs to fill His children with His overflowing, overwhelming love. This is the goal of all forgiveness: *to be filled with Christ Himself.* It is our Father's good pleasure to give us His Kingdom of righteousness, peace, joy within (Luke 12:32).

If you have an emotional need that wasn't met in childhood, for example love, attention, or approval, forgive the person who didn't give you what you needed, and release the internal demand to God. Then welcome Him to fill that area of need with His love! God delights in filling His children's hearts with what they need. He can give us what no earthly parent could ever supply!

When my father and my mother forsake me, then the LORD will take care of me. (Psalm 27:10)

The Forgiveness Lifestyle

This process of *"first-feel-forgive"* is a very fast and effective "God encounter" that you can have multiple times every hour of every day. This is what we describe as "the forgiveness lifestyle." Throughout the day, practice the Presence of God by staying "dropped down," yielding your will to

God, remaining open in your heart and basking in the peace of Christ. The *moment* any negative emotion disturbs your peace, *begin the "first, feel, forgive" process.* Forgiveness will become a habit of being, a lifestyle that you practice in order to commune with Christ without ceasing.

> ### *Learn to live a forgiveness LIFESTYLE!*

When there is adequate time, ask the Lord to show you the source of any negative emotion. Where did it get started, Lord? Begin with the FIRST person or situation that comes to mind. FEEL the feeling associated with that memory. Then FORGIVE by yielding to *Christ the Forgiver* as He flows to and through that person and situation to bring forgiveness and healing where there was wounding and offense.

It's that simple: *first, feel, forgive* throughout the day.

Pay attention to every single negative emotion that disturbs your peace in God and allow Christ the Forgiver to flow to and through that emotion. With practice you can begin to abide in Christ. As each negative feeling interrupts your *shalom,* yield your will to Christ and allow Him to do the rest.

Experiencing supernatural forgiveness is vital in your everyday life—no matter the context or occasion. Drop down to stay in peace, for example, with your family at holidays. Don't lose your peace when you're caught in a traffic jam, stuck in a long grocery line or busily making dinner, doing homework or attending a business lunch. Here are two practical examples of how to yield to Christ the Forgiver in stressful situations:

True story: *Jake's boss was yelling at him, blaming him for something his co-worker had done. Jake simply dropped down, yielded his will, released forgiveness to his boss, and immediately experienced God's peace. His co-worker later went to the boss and confessed.*

True story: *A pastor was waiting in line at the grocery store with a "crabby clerk" keeping everyone waiting. The pastor simply dropped down, yielded his will and allowed Christ the Forgiver to flow to the clerk. He experienced God's marvelous peace while the other customers were getting upset. Even more exciting, by the time he made his purchase, the clerk was actually beginning to smile.*

Review

Once again, just follow these three easy steps to experience supernatural forgiveness:

FIRST

    First person or situation. *What is the first person or situation God brings to mind—in an image or memory?*

FEEL

    Feel the feeling. *What is the emotion you feel in your gut?*

FORGIVE

    Forgive. *Yield your will and let Christ the Forgiver flow out toward the person or situation, yourself or God.*

Be mindful that these simple steps *contradict* the most common misconceptions about forgiveness:

- ✓ *Christ* is the Forgiver, so forgiveness works *every time*.
- ✓ Forgiveness is *instant,* not a process.
- ✓ There is no "big or little" offense: forgiveness is *all* easy for Jesus.

STAY CONNECTED 24/7

Communion with Christ is simply *maintaining your connection* with God.

Picture getting married to someone. You supposedly live together now, but you only let them in the door for ten minutes twice a day. They stand there on the front porch, patiently waiting all day and all night—but you just ignore them until it is convenient for you.

Who would tolerate treatment like that? That is not a *relationship*.

Communing with someone is enjoying a *real* relationship with them. When you commune, you share each other's thoughts and feelings in a profoundly close relationship. Communion is based on deep intimacy, vulnerability and transparency, sharing your being with another without restraint, fear or shame.

In John 15, Jesus invites us to *abide* in Him, stay connected with Him all the time. Communion with God is touching His Presence within our spirit—and yielding to Christ the Forgiver as soon as anything interrupts our peace.

> ***Communion is based on deep intimacy,***
> ***vulnerability and transparency, sharing***
> ***your being with another without restraint.***

In the Gospels, we learn that Jesus chose to be alone for prayer at times, but we also learn that He was in *continuous fellowship* with the Father, maintaining a spiritual connection with God in the middle of jostling crowds in the noisy marketplace:

"Then Jesus answered and said to them, "Most assuredly, I say to you, the Son can do nothing of Himself, but what He sees the Father do..." (John 5:19)

The Apostle John gives us the wonderful news that we, too, can have that same intimate communion with God. John enjoyed a relationship with Jesus during His time on earth, but he also writes that he is *still* having fellowship with Him:

"The infinite Life of God Himself took shape before us. We saw it, we heard it, and now we're telling you so you can experience it along with us, this experience of communion with the Father and His Son, Jesus Christ." (1 John 1:2-4 MSG)

We may not *talk* to God continuously, but we can learn to *touch* His Presence, spirit-to-Spirit, without interruption. It is possible to "pray without ceasing" (1 Thessalonians 5:17).

We can experience union with God moment by moment, but especially during our devotional time, as we focus only on Him, one-on-One, face-to-Face. To stay connected during the day, it is vital to *start* connected!

> **To stay connected,**
> **it is vital to start connected!**

Simple Prayer

Prayer should be simple. *Simple*—easy, uncomplicated, no mixture, undefiled, complete: nothing extra, nothing missing—*Prayer*. Nothing extra, nothing missing. Pure is a synonym of "simple". Simple Prayer is prayer focused on God alone, prayer that is *pure*, with only one aim: to adore and glorify God.

"For I am jealous for you with a godly jealousy; for I betrothed you to one husband, so that to Christ I might present you as a pure virgin. But I am afraid that, as the serpent deceived Eve by his craftiness, your minds will be led astray from the simplicity and purity of devotion to Christ." (2 Corinthians 11:2-4 NASB)

When you devote time to communing with God, come before the Lord *expecting* to meet with Him and touch or perceive His Presence. Simple Prayer. This is a *devoted time*, an offering of your time given as a holy gift to God. Present yourself to Him and yield your will. Drop down to your spirit and open that door to your heart. Remember that you are coming before God to honor and love Him. Dedicate yourself to Him as a living sacrifice.

Consider this time as time to seek God for Himself alone. Make God your number one priority! This is not the time to petition for your own needs or to intercede on behalf of others, although petitions and intercession are certainly important. The attitude of our heart is focused on pursuing loving friendship with God. This time of profound communion is the good soil where deep intimacy begins to grow.

> *As you present yourself to the Lord,*
> *know that He is giving you*
> *His undivided attention.*

Drop down, focus on Christ and allow His Presence to flood your mind, will, and emotions. As you do, expect the surroundings to "slip away" and to be so caught up with Him that you may even lose your sense of time, even though you may feel some initial resistance from your flesh. This resistance will fade as you say "no" to distractions and stretch your capacity to remain in His Presence. Small victories develop power to overcome flesh.

As the Lord gives His attention to you, also acknowledge Him as a *real Person* with you. Come before Him in reverence (Hebrews 4:13) because you have an audience with the King of kings!

When you present yourself to the Lord, know that He is giving you His undivided attention. You are His constant delight. Every time that you draw close to Him, you *ravish His heart.*

Awareness of the Lord and sensitivity to His Presence are progressive and are based on the discovery of Who God is. We take the posture of a student before the Master Teacher. We don't have anything to say until we have heard from Him (Isaiah 50:4).

> *Awareness of the Lord is progressive,*
> *based on the discovery of Who God is.*

The Holy Spirit may speak through whispers, impressions, pictures, or scripture. Be patient. Just as natural growth takes time, spiritual growth needs time to develop (Psalm 27:14). As you become accustomed to being still before the Lord, you will be able to stay in prayer for longer periods of time.

The Lord will bring any sins to your remembrance with a very gentle, loving nudge of His Spirit. His voice is never condemning or judgmental. If you hear an accusing, harsh voice in your thoughts, be assured that that is the enemy's voice sent to discourage you.

It is the goodness of the Lord that leads us to repentance. If He does bring sins to mind, yield your will and receive forgiveness, opening your heart to the "washing of the water of the Word" (Titus 3:5). Do any Scriptures come to your mind? Welcome a fresh touch, a cleansing and refreshing from the Holy Spirit.

Friendship with God

Time spent in prayer prepares you to walk as a friend of God during the day. A parent helps a child get ready for new adventures, gives him or her much needed words of wisdom, and provides loving support. Your heavenly Father knows what you will face each day, and desires to give you everything you will need to successfully navigate through life. But even more than that, He will be right there with you every step of the way! Friend with friend.

Friends genuinely care about one another. God has emotions, just like we do. He can rejoice and laugh. He celebrates the prodigal and grieves for the sinner. He is a deeply emotional Person. Nothing is more amazing or necessary in life than to intimately know this emotional, brilliant, ecstatically loving God. He is Love Himself. He loves *you*, and He wants you to love Him in return.

$$\left\{ \begin{array}{c} \textbf{\textit{God loves you, and He}} \\ \textbf{\textit{wants you to love Him in return.}} \end{array} \right\}$$

Communion with Love Himself is not a special gift for special saints or hidden knowledge for experts. Any believer, young or old, is meant to experience oneness with the Beloved.

The Lord Jesus Christ took our sins upon Himself on the Cross and rose again in victory for this unspeakably glorious access to His Presence. We are the "bride" of the Lamb (Rev. 21:9). Jesus also said, "I have called you friends" (John 15:15).

Experiencing God as a Friend is different from doing good works or making great sacrifices. It is *touching His Presence* continually, without the interference of the enemy's inroads of fear, stress or anxiety. Friendship with God is learning to abide in Christ without ceasing.

> *Jesus said,*
> *"I have called you friends."*

When God called Abraham his friend in II Chronicles 20:7 and Isaiah 41:8, the Hebrew word used is *'ahab*. This same Hebrew word is also translated *lover* or "one who is loving and beloved, intimate; different from a companion." This Hebrew term *ahab* also means "to desire, to breathe after." Imagine: this intimate "breathing after" described Abraham's friendship with God!

Moses was also called a friend of God (Exodus 33:11), but the Hebrew term used in this Exodus passage is *rea`*, translated "companion" or "neighbor." Moses was a neighbor or companion of God, whereas Abraham was God's beloved, His intimate one. Abraham had a deeper *degree* of intimacy.

Because of the Cross, our degree of intimacy with God is even greater than Abraham's. Unlike Abraham, we have the Spirit of Christ within us. Before the Cross, the Holy Spirit could not indwell believers. Now, because of the glorious Cross and resurrection, we are *one with Christ*.

> *True bliss is touching God's Presence*
> *with every breath we breathe.*

The Lord's invitation to His followers is simple and clear: *"Abide in me, and I in you"* (John 15:4). With consistent and diligent practice, we can learn to experience His mind with our thoughts. We can experience His emotions with the emotions we feel. We can encounter His dominion, His Kingdom, with the actions we will to do, in perfect harmony with His will.

We can learn to become wholly yielded vessels of Love.

This is true friendship with God, the bliss of touching His Presence with every breath we breathe.

"If you look for me wholeheartedly, you will find me. I will be found by you," says the Lord..." (Jeremiah 29:13-14a NLT)

BIBLIOGRAPHY

Anderson, N.B. & Anderson, P.E. (2003). *Emotional Longevity: what really determines how long you live*. New York, NY: Viking.

Barefoot, J. et al (1984). "Hostility CHD Incidence in Total Mortality - A Twenty-Five Year Follow-Up Study of Twenty Five Physicians". Psychosomatic Medicine, 45: 79-83.

Baum, A. & Polsusnzy, D. (1999). "Health Psychology: Mapping Biobehavioral Contributions to Health and Illness". Annual Review of Psychology, Vol. 50, 137-163.

Lawrence, Brother (2010). 1692. *The Practice of the Presence of God*. Brewster, MA: Paraclete Press. (Originally published as a brief booklet shortly after Lawrence's death in 1691).

Cohen, S. et al. (2007). "Psychological Stress and Disease". Journal of the American Medical Association (JAMA) 2007; 298(14): 1685-1687.

Colbert, D. (2003). *Deadly Emotions*. Nashville, TN: Thomas Nelson Publishers.

Dennerstein L, Lehert P, Burger H, Dudley E. (1999). "Factors affecting sexual functioning of women in the mid-life years". Climacteric. 1999;2:254–62.

Gershon, M. (2003). *The Second Brain*. New York, NY; HarperCollins. (Original work published 1999).

Gross, J., & Levenson, R. (1997). "Hiding feelings: The acute effects of inhibiting positive and negative emotions". Journal of Abnormal Psychology, 106, 95-103.

Jensen, M. (1987). "Psychobiological factors predicting the course of breast cancer". Journal of Personality, 55, 317-342.

Larzelere, M.M. and Jones, G.N. (2008). "Stress and Health". Primary Care: Clinics in Office Practice. 2008;35(4):839-856.

Lawler K., Younger J., Piferi R., Billington E, Jobe R, Edmondson K, Jones W.H. (2003). "A change of heart: cardiovascular correlates of forgiveness in response to interpersonal conflict". Journal of Behavioral Medicine, 26, 373-393.

Lawler K., Younger J., Piferi R., Jobe R., Edmondson K., Jones W. (2005). "The unique effects of forgiveness on health: an exploration of pathways". Journal of Behavioral Medicine, 28, 157-167.

Matè, G. (2003). *When the Body Says No: Understanding the Stress-Disease Connection.* Hoboken, NJ: John Wiley & Sons, Inc. (Original work published in Canada 2003).

Parischa, P. (2005). "The stomach cannot lie". New Scientist. Magazine, issue 2524, 05.

Parischa, P. (2008). "Lie detection via electrogastrography". US2008/0177157 A1. Houston, Texas.

Pert, C. (2003). *Molecules of Emotion: the Science Behind Mind-Body Medicine.* New York, NY: Scribner. (Original work published 1997).

Pennebaker, J. (1992). "Inhibition as the linchpin of health". In H. S. Friedman (Ed.), Hostility, coping, and health. Washington, DC: American Psychological Association. 127-139.

Sarno, J. (1998). *The Mindbody Prescription: Healing the Body, Healing the Pain.* New York, NY: Wellness Central, Hatchette Book Group.

Temoshok, L. (1987). "Personality, coping style, emotion, and cancer: Towards an integrative model". Cancer Surveys, 6, 545-567.

Vgontzas, A.N. et al. (1997). "Chronic insomnia and activity of the stress system: a preliminary study". Journal of Psychosomatic Research, Vol. 45, 21-31.

Zautra, A. (2003). *Emotions, Stress, and Health.* New York, NY: Oxford University Press, Inc.

Worthington, E.L., Jr., Berry, J.W., & Parrott, L. III (2001). "Unforgiveness, forgiveness, religion, and health". In T. G. Plante & A.C. Sherman (Eds.), Faith and health: Psychological perspectives. New York: Guilford Press, 107-138.

ABOUT THE AUTHORS

As a pastor and church planter, Dennis Clark has been in ministry for more than 30 years. Dr. Jennifer Clark, B.S, M.S., Ed.S., Th.D., is a psychologist and pastor. They minister together full-time as a husband and wife team.

Dennis and Dr. Jen have developed simple, systematic, proven how-to tools to set people free from emotional pain and equip them to teach it to others. They provide simple keys easy enough for a mom or Sunday school worker to teach a 3 year old child, yet effective enough to heal the deepest hurts of adults quickly and completely.

The Clarks founded Full Stature Ministries and Kingdom Life Church, located in Fort Mill, South Carolina. They also direct TEAM Embassy, a Training Embassy for Advanced Ministry.

For video demonstrations and further teachings:

www.forgive123.com

www.kingdomlifechurch.us